A BLESSING OF
Music

WELLERAN POLTARNEES

LAUGHING ELEPHANT   MMIII

LAUGHING ELEPHANT BOOKS
3645 INTERLAKE AVENUE NORTH   SEATTLE   98103

WWW.LAUGHINGELEPHANT.COM

I AM GRATEFUL
FOR THE GLORIOUS GIFT
OF MUSIC

A BLESSING OF *Music*

It brings us into closer harmony
with the universe,

A BLESSING OF *Music*

and with our deepest selves.

A BLESSING OF *Music*

Music connects us to others –

7

A BLESSING OF *Music*

its creators,

A BLESSING OF *Music*

the performers,

A BLESSING OF *Music*

and those who share the music with us.

A BLESSING OF *Music*

Music lifts us out of ourselves,

letting us forget our daily cares.

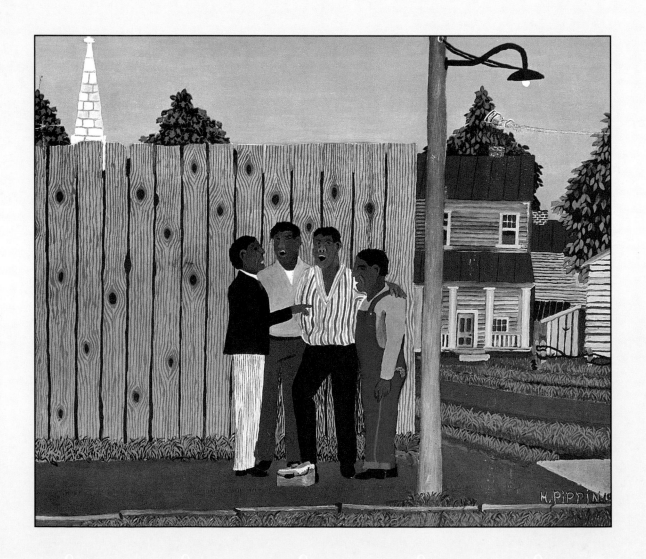

A BLESSING OF *Music*

It is a language for feelings
that have no other expression,

19

A BLESSING OF *Music*

and is universal in its appeal.

A BLESSING OF  *Music*

Music requires
harmonious cooperation.

A BLESSING OF *Music*

It is healing and life enriching.

A BLESSING OF *Music*

Music enlivens the imagination,

A BLESSING OF *Music*

and fills us with a mysterious joy.

29

A BLESSING OF *Music*

Music reminds us continually
of the possibility of perfection,

A BLESSING OF *Music*

and is always a nearby
opportunity for happiness.

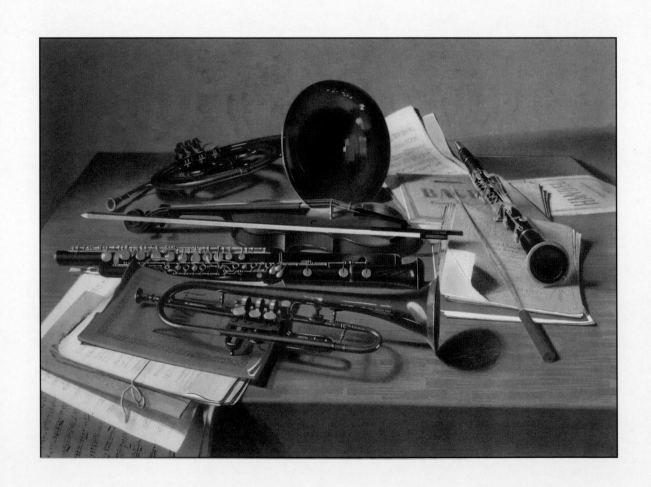

PICTURE CREDITS